Buying a Used Car in the UK:

Avoid Scams and Find the Best Deals

By

Jim Starling

Disclaimer

The information provided in this book is for general informational purposes only. The author and publisher make no representations or warranties of any kind, express or implied, about the completeness, accuracy, reliability, suitability or availability with respect to the information, products, services, or related graphics contained in this book for any purpose. Any reliance you place on such information is therefore strictly at your own risk.

In no event will the author or publisher be liable for any loss or damage including without limitation, indirect or consequential loss or damage, or any loss or damage whatsoever arising from loss of data, money, or profits arising out of, or in connection with, the use of this book.

The information contained in this book is not intended as a substitute for professional advice and should not be relied upon in the absence of such professional advice. Always seek the advice of a qualified professional before making any decisions related to buying a used car or making financial decisions.

The author and publisher make no representations or warranties that the information contained in this book is correct or that it will help you find the perfect used car or guarantee a successful transaction.

The views and opinions expressed in this book are those of the author and do not necessarily reflect the official policy or position of any other agency, organization, employer or company.

This book is for entertainment and informational purposes only. The author and publisher shall have neither liability nor responsibility to any person or entity with respect to any loss or damage caused or alleged to be caused directly or indirectly by the information contained in this book.

Foreword

My name is Jim Starling, I am the presenter, writer, editor, camera operator, director and tea boy of a YouTube automotive channel "DefinitelyNotAGuru" and freelance motoring writer, presenter and content maker.

In 2021, I made the bold, or maybe stupid, decision to quit the corporate life and make a huge change. I began building a new career, a large part of which just had to quench my thirst for cars; not supercars, not special cars – just cars. I'm someone who enjoys the ordinary just as much as the extra-ordinary and I really love to take a deep dive into the business and industry behind the product.

My lifelong passion for cars has only ever been equalled by my desire to always find a great deal on everything from my TV to my holiday…and yes…my cars. I'm often found searching classified ads for cars that I don't want/need or reading up on common faults of cars I have no intention of owning. Yes, I'm a nerdy sad case who simply loves all things automotive.

I've had more cars than most, on more than one occasion I have been contacted by DVLA to see if I am a motor trader as I've changed cars so frequently. I also ran a company fleet for several years which opened my eyes to the world of leasing, something that has become a specialist subject of mine.

Since launching the YouTube channel and my website https://notaguru.co.uk. I've become a different person, being genuinely fulfilled by what I do rather than dedicating my life to something that had more of a negative impact on me than a positive one – although it did pay quite a lot better! What I've always wanted to do more than anything is to feel that I've helped someone – that may sound cheesy but it's true.

My YouTube channel has lots of content related to buying used vehicles, from best used car buys and leasing deals to consumer advice and scam alerts. I've been asked literally hundreds of times to write a guide that attempts to help used car buyers navigate their way through all the jargon and the scammers whilst giving hints and tips on what to look out for and where. It seems I ran out of excuses not to start writing and now we find ourselves here.

I can't thank you enough for buying my guide and I truly hope that it helps you make a great decision with your next car; I have tried to make it concise, to the point and free from "waffle" – I hope I succeeded and hope that you have years of trouble-free motoring ahead.

Table of Contents

CHAPTER 1:

Introduction to the UK Used Car Market

Welcome to my guide on buying a used car in the UK.

If you're reading this, chances are you're in the market for a new (used) car and want some help navigating what can be shark infested waters. But before you go running off to your nearest dealership or start browsing online classifieds, it's important to understand the used car market.

The used car market in the UK is a large and vibrant one, with a wide variety of options available for buyers. According to the Society of Motor Manufacturers and Traders (SMMT), in 2020, the used car market in the UK was worth over £80 billion, with around 8 million used cars sold in the country.

The market is diverse, with a range of options available for buyers, including cars from different manufacturers, different price ranges and different age groups. There are also various types of sellers, including professional motor traders, private sellers and online marketplaces.

One of the major trends in the UK used car market is the shift towards online sales. With the advent of online marketplaces and digital tools, it has become easier for buyers to research and purchase used cars online. This trend has accelerated during the COVID-19 pandemic as people are more inclined to buy vehicles without physical contact.

There is a growing popularity for battery powered electric and hybrid cars at the time of writing, with diesel cars becoming far less attractive on the used market. As the technology for battery vehicles improves and the infrastructure for charging expands, more and more buyers are looking for used electric and hybrid cars. There are currently (Jan 2023) around 660,000 EVs on UK roads and it is projected that this number will reach 6.5 million by 2030.

The UK used car market is heavily influenced by the new car market. When new cars are in high demand (or short supply), used car prices tend to go up and vice versa. During the pandemic we've seen some of the highest car prices in the UK, the war in Ukraine has also affected prices due to its effect on the supply chain of some new car parts.

It's important to understand the difference between a "Manufacturer Approved Used" or "Certified Pre-Owned" (CPO) vehicle and a regular used car. A CPO vehicle is a used car that has been thoroughly inspected, reconditioned by a manufacturer or dealership and often comes with an extended manufacturer warranty or other benefits. While CPO vehicles tend to be more expensive than regular used cars, they can offer peace of mind for buyers who want to minimize the risk of buying a vehicle with hidden problems.

Another thing to consider when buying a used car is the vehicle's history. A car's history can have a big influence on its price/value. Information about a car's past, such as whether it has been subject to an insurance write-off for example, can be found through a vehicle history report, which can be obtained from various companies such as Vcheck or Car Vertical. More on this in Chapter 6 – it can be a real eye opener!

The UK used car market is highly competitive, with many dealers and private sellers vying for the attention of buyers. As a result, it's important to do your research and shop around to get the best deal possible.

I strongly suggest you read this guide form start to finish before you even start searching for a car. Some of this you will already know but there is plenty to learn along the way. Start your search well informed and you'll save a lot of time, effort and maybe even some money!

Did you know that the average age of a used car sold in the UK is around 7 years? This means that many used cars on the market have already been through multiple owners and have a fair amount of mileage on the clock.

Now that you have a basic understanding of the dynamic landscape of UK used car market, it's time to move on.

CHAPTER 2:

UK Motor Trade Terminology, Jargon & Slang

The UK motor trade is a world of its own, with its own set of terms, phrases and jargon that can be confusing for those not in the know. If you're new to the industry or just looking to buy or sell a car, understanding the lingo can be the key to making informed decisions and getting the best deal. From "MOT" and "service history" to "trade price" and "book price", this article will provide you with a comprehensive guide to the most used jargon in the UK motor trade. Whether you're a seasoned veteran or a newbie, you're sure to learn something new and valuable. So, let's dive in and demystify the world of UK motor trade jargon!

Here are 30 common words and phrases that may help answer some questions for you along the way when navigating this guide and finding your next car:

1. **Service History:** The service book and receipts and other supporting documentation used to verify the maintenance record of the car.

2. **Trade plates:** These are special license plates that are used by motor trade professionals to temporarily register a vehicle while it is being driven for business purposes.

3. **Cherished Plate / Private Plate:** A personalised registration number that is considered valuable, this type of registration plate is often used as a status symbol

4. **HPI check**: HPI stands for "Hire Purchase Inspection" and it's a service that provides information about a vehicle's history, such as whether it has been reported stolen, has outstanding finance, or has been in an accident.

5. **MOT:** This stands for "Ministry of Transport" test, an annual test to ensure vehicles meet the minimum safety and environmental standards in the UK.

6. **Trade Sale:** This refers to a sale of a vehicle between two traders, as opposed to a retail sale to a private individual. Trade sales are generally made without comeback or warranty.

7. **Book price:** The price of a vehicle of this age/mileage/condition according to a trade price guide such as Glass's or Cap HPI.

8. **Stock:** A term used to describe the vehicles that are currently available for sale at a dealership.

9. **Part-ex / trade-in:** short for "part-exchange" is when a customer trades in their old car in order to get a discount on a new car.

10. **ABS:** Anti-lock brakes, designed to prevent skidding when heavy braking is used.

11. **Banger / Lemon / Beater:** A term used to describe an older or worn-out car that is in poor condition.

12. **ICE:** In car entertainment the Stereo, Navigation, Infotainment etc

13. **Car Finance / PCP / PCH / HP :** All ways of borrowing to pay for a car, more on this in the car finance chapter.

14. **Deposit Contribution / Dealer contribution:** Offered by the manufacturer to customers when buying a car, usually new, on finance. This sum is discounted from the overall finance package, whether it's a hire purchase (HP) or personal contract plan (PCP). It's only available when buying the vehicle through the manufacturer's own finance service. Not always as good as it seems!

15. **Dealer prep:** The preparation work that a dealership does on a vehicle before it is sold, such as cleaning and detailing, safety checks and any necessary repairs.

16. **Showroom condition:** A term used to describe a vehicle that is in excellent condition, as if it were still in a dealership showroom.

17. **Depreciation:** the difference between what you pay for a car today and what it's worth in a few years' time when you sell it.

18. **GMFV:** The Guaranteed Minimum Future Value (GMFV) is the finance company's estimate of what a car will be worth, taking account of depreciation, at the end of a PCP contract. It's the amount you will have to pay if you want to 'buy' the car at the end of the PCP.

19. **Bent / Moody:** Not what it appears to be, false, fake.

20. **Pre-Registered:** A pre-reg' vehicle is one registered by a dealer, first owner listed on registration. These vehicles may offer cost savings but have limited selection in colours, features and specifications. They are usually bought by dealers to meet sales targets and earn manufacturer bonuses.

21. **Write-off:** An insurance "total loss", where the insurer pays out the policyholder for the value of their car following a theft, accident dame, fire or flood etc where the car is not recovered or uneconomical/unviable to repair.

22. **Trade price:** The price at which a dealership will buy a vehicle from another dealership or a trade seller.

23. **Trade-in allowance:** The amount of money that a dealership will offer a customer for their old car as a trade-in.

24. **Insurance Group:** This helps give you an idea of how easy or cheap it may be to insure a vehicle, the lower the group the cheaper the insurance is the basic theory. Lower insured grouped cars can also be easier for young or inexperienced drivers to insure.

25. **Trade Sale:** Sold "as-seen" without warranty or comeback.

26. **ULEZ:** Ultra Low Emissions Zone, some towns and cities have an ULEZ area, this is an area where card that are determined to be "unclean" are either not allowed to enter or must pay a fee in order to enter that zone. These zones are likely to become more prevalent in future.

27. **MPG:** Miles Per Gallon – this is how fuel efficient a car is. If you see WLTP next to this figure it's usually more accurate than results from cars that have been tested to different standards.

28. **Ex-demo:** When allowing potential customers to test drive vehicles, dealerships use cars known as demonstrator vehicles. These vehicles, if sold, can be priced less expensively than brand new models with the same specifications.

29. **Gap Insurance:** This is intended to fill the gap between the amount your insurance company will pay out for a write-off and the remaining balance on your finance agreement. Often sold alongside a Lease (PCP or PCH) or Hire Purchase Agreement.

30. **Road Tax, VED:** In the UK, "road tax" is officially known as "vehicle excise duty" (VED). It is a tax that must be paid annually for most vehicles that are used on public roads. The amount of VED that must be paid is based on the vehicle's emissions and fuel type.

CHAPTER 3:

Setting a Budget and Determining Your Needs

When buying a used car, one of the most important steps is to set a budget and determine what you actually need in a car. Buying a used car can be a great way to save money, but it's important to go into the process with a clear idea of how much you can afford to spend, so you don't end up overspending.

First, look at your finances and determine a realistic budget for your used car purchase. This should include not just the purchase price of the car, but also any additional costs such as taxes and insurance. Keep in mind that buying a used car can come with unexpected costs, such as repairs or maintenance, so it's important to factor that into your budget as well. If you have £10,000 to spend on a car, consider only spending say £9,000 and keeping £1,000 as a "rainy day fund" in-case you get unforeseen problems with the car.

Next, take a look at your current transportation needs. Are you looking for a car to commute to work or school? Are you in need of a larger vehicle to accommodate your growing family? Do you need a car with specific features such as a sunroof or a certain type of engine? These are all important considerations when determining your needs.

It's also important to consider the vehicle's age and mileage. Generally, the newer the car and the lower the mileage, the more expensive it will be. However, it's important to remember that a car's age and mileage are not the only indicators of its condition. A well-maintained car with high mileage can be a better purchase than a poorly maintained car with low mileage.

Do you live in an Ultra-Low Emission Zone or is your town or city likely to be getting one any time soon? If so, think about ULEZ compliant vehicle (more on this later!).

Another factor to consider is fuel efficiency. If you plan on using the car for a daily commute, consider a car that has a good fuel economy to save money on gas in the long run.

Lastly, consider the car's safety features. Look for cars with safety features such as airbags, anti-lock brakes and stability control as well as looking at crash test ratings.

Once you've taken all of these factors into consideration, you should have a better idea of what you can afford and what you're looking for in a used car. Remember that setting a budget and determining your needs is a crucial step in the used car buying process, as it will help you to narrow down your search and make a more informed decision.

Another important thing to consider when setting a budget is the car's insurance cost. Different makes and models have different insurance rates. It's important to research the insurance rates of the cars you're considering before making a purchase. This will give you a more accurate picture of the total cost of owning the car.

Additionally, consider the long-term cost of ownership. This includes things like fuel, maintenance and repairs. Some cars are known to have higher maintenance costs than others. Researching the long-term cost of ownership of the cars you're considering can also help you make a more informed decision.

It's also a good idea to consider the resale value of the car you're considering. Cars that hold their value well are often a better investment than cars that depreciate quickly.

Once you've settled on a car (or maybe a few different makes and models) to search for, do a little bit of research, a quick online search of "2010 Ford Focus common issues" will bring up plenty of information. Repeat this for any cars you're considering, sometimes this will scare you off but sometimes it just makes you aware of things that you should be looking out for when viewing a vehicle. Online forums can also be a great source of owner knowledge, most makes and models of cars have a forum and they tend to have members only too willing to help.

All in all, setting a budget and determining your needs is an important step in the used car buying process. It allows you to focus your search, make more informed decisions and ultimately find a car that meets your needs and fits your budget.

CHAPTER 4:

Buying a Used Car from a Professional Motor Trader in the UK

O ne of the options available to you is purchasing from a professional motor trader. These traders, also known as car dealerships, specialise in buying and selling used cars and can offer a variety of benefits to buyers.

One of the biggest advantages of buying from a professional motor trader is the level of service and expertise they sometimes provide. These traders should have a wealth of knowledge about the cars they sell and can provide valuable information and advice to buyers. They can often also help buyers with financing and insurance options, although not always at the most competitive terms.

Another benefit of buying from a professional motor trader is the required level of transparency and accountability. Unlike private sellers, professional traders are regulated by the UK government and are required to abide by certain rules and regulations. This means that buyers can have more confidence in the car they are purchasing and can be sure that the trader has provided accurate information about the car's condition and history.

Your Rights when buying from a Motor Trader in the UK

Under the Consumer Rights Act 2015, if a fault renders the product not of satisfactory quality, not fit for purpose or not as described, then the buyer is entitled to reject it within the first 30 days. If a fault comes to light after 30 days but before 6 months you're entitled to a repair, replacement, or refund. It's assumed in law that the fault was present at the time of purchase unless the seller can prove otherwise. *Satisfactory quality means that the vehicle should be of a standard a reasonable person would expect, considering its age, value, history, mileage and description.*

Unless you've agreed otherwise, the dealer has only one opportunity to repair or replace the faulty vehicle after which, if they fail to repair it, you're entitled to a refund.

In the event of a refund following a failed attempt at repair during the first six months the seller may make a 'reasonable' adjustment to the amount refunded to take account of the use that you've had of the vehicle.

After 6 months the burden is on you to prove that the product was faulty at the time of delivery if you want to pursue a claim for repair or replacement.

It is also worth noting that, under the Road Traffic Act 1988, no person can sell a motor vehicle or trailer in an unroadworthy condition.

When buying from a professional motor trader, it's important to do your research and shop around to find the best deals. Look for traders that have a good reputation and be sure to read reviews and testimonials from previous customers. It's also important to thoroughly inspect the car before making a purchase and to ask the trader any questions you may have about the car's condition and history, get the responses in writing for extra peace of mind. Always ask your questions and get your responses BEFORE you agree to purchase a car.

Most professional motor traders in the UK offer warranties on their vehicles. This means that in case of any issues with the vehicle after purchase, the trader should take the responsibility of fixing it. This can be a great way to protect yourself against unexpected costs. *More about this in chapter 7!*

One thing to keep in mind when buying a used car from a professional motor trader is that the prices tend to be higher than buying from a private seller, as these traders have considerable overhead costs and themselves take on a degree of risk as you have rights and they also must make a profit of course.

Buying a used car from a professional motor trader in the UK can offer several benefits, including a wide selection of cars to choose from, expert advice and a level of transparency and accountability. However, it's important to do your research, thoroughly inspect the car and be aware of the potential higher prices and unwanted sales tactics.

CHAPTER 5:

Buying a Used Car from a Private Seller in the UK

Another option available to you is purchasing from a private seller. This can be a great way to find a good deal on a car, but it also comes with its own set of risks and challenges.

One of the biggest advantages of buying from a private seller is the potential for a lower price. Since private sellers are not operating a business, they may be more willing to negotiate on the price of the car. Additionally, private sellers often have personal connections to the car and may be more willing to provide detailed information about its history and condition.

Buying a car from a private seller allows you to avoid the pressure of salespeople trying to upsell you on a more expensive car or additional services but private sellers come in all sorts of flavours; just look at the cast of characters walking down your local High Street, from the sharply dressed older gentleman with a broadsheet newspaper under his arm, to the young family of 4, to the man dressed only in tracksuit bottoms and an ankle tag vomiting into his cider outside a pub at 11:00am – a private seller could be anyone. It's always wise to take a friend or family member with you when viewing a car.

Private sellers rarely prepare their cars for sale in the same way that a dealership would, this can something give the car a more genuine appearance than one that has undergone the full 'dealership treatment' this comes with its own set of pros and cons. Being able to see an engine bay that has not been professionally cleaned is a good place to start as you'll often be able to spot signs of historic fluid leaks and ageing parts than in a car that has had the engine bay steam cleaned and dressed. The downside is that the engine bay may be quite grubby, the interior may be looking a little tired and there are bound to be some scuffs and scrapes on the bodywork and wheels. All these small things can have a big influence of your perceived value of the car you are looking and is something to be aware of. £2/300 spent on preparation can often take an old tired looking car and make it look as young and vibrant as a showroom car.

However, buying from a private seller also comes with some risks. One of the biggest risks is that the car may have hidden issues that the seller is not aware of or is not disclosing. It's important to thoroughly inspect the car before making a purchase and to ask the seller any questions you may have about the car's condition and history. A vehicle history report can also be obtained to verify the car's history.

Another risk when buying from a private seller is that there may be no legal protection in case of any issues after purchase. Unlike buying from a professional trader, private sellers are not regulated by the UK government and may not be so easily held accountable for any inaccuracies in the information provided about the car.

It's also important to be aware of scams when buying from a private seller. Scammers may use fake advertisements or fraudulent documents to trick buyers into buying a car that does not exist or has serious issues. Be sure to thoroughly research the seller and the car before making a purchase and be wary of any deals that seem too good to be true.

When buying from a private seller, it's important to have all the necessary paperwork in order. This includes the car's registration documents, the V5C logbook and the MOT certificate. Also make sure you're buying from the address on the V5 rather than a pub car park or "his mate's house".

Just remember that whilst buying a used car from a private seller in the UK can offer the potential for a lower price, it's not without risk.

CHAPTER 6:

The Importance of a Vehicle History Report in the UK

When buying a used car in the UK, a Vehicle History Report (VHR) can provide valuable information about the car's past and help you make an informed decision. A VHR can give you insight into the car's history, such as whether it's been in any accidents, if it has a clear title, if it has been reported stolen or if it has outstanding finance.

A VHR can be obtained from various providers in the UK and it's a good idea to have one before making a final decision on a used car. The report will provide you with a detailed account of the car's history, including information on:

- Number of previous owners

- MOT history and advisories

- Mileage history

- Outstanding finance

- If the car has been reported stolen

- If the car has been recorded as written off

- If the car has been imported

- If the car has been used as a Taxi

- Any recorded accident history

- VIN number check

- Has the car ever been through a salvage auction? (this is a big one!)

This information can help you identify any potential issues with the car and can give you a more accurate picture of the car's condition and history. It's especially important to have a VHR if you're buying a car from a private seller, as they may not have all the information about the car's history.

It's important to note that a VHR is not a substitute for a mechanical inspection and it's still recommended to have a professional mechanic inspect the car before making a final decision. A VHR can give you valuable information about the car's history, but it cannot guarantee the car's mechanical condition.

A Vehicle History Report can provide valuable information about a used car's past and can help you make an informed decision when buying a used car in the UK. It's important to have one before making a final decision, especially when buying from a private seller. However, it's still important to have a professional mechanical inspection, a VHR is not a substitute for a thorough inspection of the car's mechanical condition. Additionally, it's important to keep in mind that not all providers of VHRs are created equal, so it's important to research and choose a reputable provider.

Please excuse the shameless plug but the main video on my YouTube Channel "DefinitelyNotAGuru" exposes the importance of choosing your history check provider very carefully. In the video we see how some of the largest providers of vehicle history checks in the UK completely miss cars that have been written-off due to accident damage but unrecorded on the main insurance database. We see examples of cars before and after damage appearing, completely legally, as "HPI Clear" in their marketing and via some very reputable sales sites. You simply MUST make your own checks before buying with a trusted company, I show you my choice of provider in that video and really suggest anyone reading this takes time to watch the video.

Buying a car with outstanding finance can be a disaster if the car is sold to you with finance against it the finance company can simply come and take the car from you as it was never the seller's property to sell in the

16

first place. The car remains the property of the finance company until any finance is settled.

A vehicle history check should be considered as part of a comprehensive evaluation of a used car and should be used in conjunction with other methods of evaluating the car such as test driving, inspecting the car, inspecting (and validating) its documentation and having it checked by a qualified mechanic.

Don't skip this step, don't trust green ticks on websites or the phrase "HPI Clear"; around £10 can potentially prevent a big mistake and save you thousands of pounds.

CHAPTER 7:

Understanding Used Car Warranties in the UK

One of the things that you may be offered by professional motor traders and even some private sellers, is a warranty.

A warranty is a guarantee that the vehicle will be free from defects in materials and workmanship for a certain period or mileage. But before you decide if it's worth it to purchase a warranty, it's important to understand how they work and the potential challenges of making a claim.

First, it's important to know that there are different types of warranties available in the UK. Some warranties are offered by the manufacturer and are transferable to the new owner, while others are offered by the dealer or a third-party company. Manufacturer warranties may be more comprehensive and offer more protection than dealer or third-party warranties.

When considering a warranty, it's important to read the fine print and understand the terms and conditions. This includes what is covered, what is not covered and any exclusions or limitations. It's also important to know the duration of the warranty and if the warranty is valid for the entire time you expect to own the car.

Another thing to consider is the cost of the warranty. Warranties vary in price and it's important to compare the cost to the potential cost of repairs or maintenance that could be covered by the warranty. Some warranties may also require the car to be serviced at certain intervals or by certain mechanics in order to remain valid, so it's important to factor in the cost of these services as well.

When it comes to making a claim, it's important to understand the process and any potential challenges. In some cases, making a claim may be straightforward and easy, but in other cases, it may be difficult and time-consuming. It's important to know who to contact and what documentation is required in order to make a claim. It's also important to understand if the car needs to go to a specific approved repairer or if any VAT registered garage can undertake repairs.

Some warranties may have a high excess, or deductible, this is the first part of any claim that is paid by you, for example a £500 repair with a £300 excess would only pay you £200), meaning that you will have to pay a certain amount out of pocket before the warranty covers the cost of the repair. Additionally, some warranties may only cover certain types of repairs or have limitations regarding the extend of repair they will cover – it's important to know that a warranty may not cover the full cost of the repairs and many third-party warranties can be far less attractive in practice than they initially appear to be on paper.

In summary, used car warranties can offer peace of mind and protection against unexpected repairs or maintenance costs, however, it's important to thoroughly understand the terms and conditions of the warranty, the cost, the quality of service and the process of making a claim. It's also important to factor in the potential challenges, such as high excesses, limitations on coverage, or restrictions on repairers when determining if a warranty is going to provide the peace of mind and value that you expect.

CHAPTER 8:

Checking the Condition of a Used Car

It's important to thoroughly inspect the vehicle to ensure that it's in good condition. This includes checking the tyres, engine, gearbox, oil, bodywork and test driving the car. In this chapter, we'll go over each of these steps in detail, so you know what to look out for when inspecting a used car.

First and foremost, checking the tyre tread is an important step. Tyre tread is the part of the tyre that comes into contact with the road and it's responsible for providing traction and handling. The legal minimum tread depth for a car tyre in the UK is 1.6mm, but ideally, you should look for a tread depth of at least 3mm. To check the tread depth, you can use a tread depth gauge or simply insert a 20p coin into the tread. If the outer band of the coin is visible, the tread depth is below the legal limit and the tyres should be replaced. It's also important to examine the tyre walls, look for cracking, rips, tears. If the tyre walls are not in good condition, then they could be at risk of blowing out, something that can be very dangerous.

Next, it's important to check the engine oil. Engine oil is crucial for lubricating the engine and keeping it running smoothly. To check the oil, locate the dipstick, pull it out and wipe it clean. Then reinsert it and pull it out again to check the oil level. The oil should be between the minimum and maximum marks on the dipstick. It's also important to check the colour and consistency of the oil. If the oil is dirty or has a milky appearance, it could be a sign of a problem with the engine, such as a head gasket leak.

It's also essential to examine the bodywork of the car. This includes checking for any dents, scratches, or rust on the exterior. Additionally, make sure to check for any signs of crash damage, such as mismatched paint or body panel gaps that aren't aligned properly. These could indicate that the car has been in an accident, which may affect its performance and safety. Check under the carpet in the boot and under the bonnet to look for panel damage or rust. Look under the car and look for excessive rust and look at the condition of the exhaust.

Check all the electrical gadgets such as mirrors, windows, door locks, stereo, interior lights, parking sensors, air conditioning, power sunroof etc, these may seem trivial but can be costly to repair or replace.

Also, pay attention to the car's warning lights, check that all the gauges are working properly and that the car is not overheating.

Verifying a car's mileage

This subject deserves more than a brief explanation and I hope it gives you some tips to help you understand if a vehicle is showing a genuine mileage or not.

It's just too easy to do these days, basically someone plugs in a laptop, works their magic, loses the service history and a car with 128,000 miles now only has 49,500.

A common thing that people say is that "it's not a problem if it's been clocked, those engines will do 200,000 miles etc", whilst that may be true in some cases you must think about the lifespan of every other component in the car. A vehicle showing an artificially low mileage may be dure for the timing belt or chain to be replaced or for the automatic gearbox to be serviced but as you are blissfully unaware these kind of maintenance jobs can be missed and can lead to devastating consequences.

There are several things to keep an eye out for to ensure the mileage on the car you're interested in.

1. The MOT history of the car should show a consistent increase year after year in most cases, you may notice a change in annual mileage once a new owner took over the car or during the pandemic but if look for irregularities in the usage pattern. Many clocked cars show very few miles added at each MOT for the past few years.

2. Beware of cars that have done 99.500 miles or 49,500 miles – the

classifieds are littered with cars that have done just a fraction under a big search filter limit; it may be a coincidence of course but there are just so many that it seems a little fishy.

3. Beware of cars with no service history or a service book with stamps but no receipts or invoices. Take the mileage shown on the odometer with a pinch of salt.

Always check a car's MOT history, you can check this for free at https://www.gov.uk/check-mot-history or get this information as part of a good Vehicle History Check service.

The test drive

Test driving the car is an important step in determining the condition of a used car.

First thing is to feel the car bonnet, is the engine already warm? This may be a sign that the owner has got it up to temperature in readiness for your arrival, it could be nothing but perhaps it doesn't like cold starts?

Start the car up, is it hesitant or does it fire up straight away? Can you hear any knocking, squeaking, or tapping noises?

During the test drive, pay attention to how the car handles and make sure all the systems are working properly. Check the brakes, steering, suspension. Listen for any unusual noises or vibrations and pay attention to how the car accelerates, brakes and handles. Look for excessive smoking from the exhaust on idle or under harsh acceleration. Does the car pull to one side when driving down the road normally or during hard braking?

Keep the stereo off for this and drive with the windows up for a little while and then with them down for a while. Try and concentrate on what you feel and hear.

For cars with a manual gearbox make sure the clutch performs as it should and that the car goes up and down through the gears without jerkiness, vibration, or juddering. For those with automatic gearboxes to do the same, try and get the car up to temperature and go between D N and R and low speed, then go on a run and try and go up and down the gears as much as possible, always keeping any eye out for jerkiness or dim-witted changes. Make sure that the automatic transmission had been serviced in line with manufacturer schedules too.

It's also important to test the car in different driving conditions, such as at motorway speed, in stop-and-go traffic and in tight turns. This will help you get a better sense of how the car handles under different conditions and can help you identify any potential issues.

If possible, have a mechanic or a trusted person inspect the car before making a final decision. A professional mechanic can identify any issues that may not be visible to the untrained eye and provide an unbiased opinion on the condition of the car.

Buying a used battery electric vehicle or hybrid vehicle

Just like other modern devices that use advanced battery packs such as smartphones or laptops, electric cars also require proper maintenance for their batteries. Although battery packs do not often malfunction, they do lose their efficiency over time which results in a shorter driving range. Replacing an electric vehicle battery pack is not as complicated as installing a new engine, but it is a very costly process that should always be handled by specialist professionals.

A very basic, but not entirely accurate way to find out the battery life of an electric vehicle (EV) is to reset the trip computer, charge it to full capacity and then check the car's computer for the estimated range. If the car was rated for 150 miles of range when it was new, but the computer now estimates only 100 miles on a full charge, this means the battery has decreased to about two-thirds of its original capacity. There are other factors that drive the estimated range such as temperature, recent driving (i.e. outside temperature, short trips, long trips, hard acceleration etc) that can have a big influence on expected range also.

Main dealerships or independent electric car specialists can give you even more information. They can do a more intensive diagnosis of battery health with the use of specialist software.

It's also worth checking to see if the battery has any manufacturer's warranty remaining, this is usually separate to the main vehicle warranty.

In summary

This is the most important part of the car buying journey for most of us yet it is often forgotten by buyers once the shiny new car is in front of them.

By paying attention to these details, you can gain a better understanding of the car's condition and identify any potential issues, this may lead you to walking away from the car or perhaps negotiating repairs or a discount before going ahead with the purchase. I would always recommend that you have a professional inspection of the car before making a final decision, to ensure that you're making a sound purchase.

Used Car Inspection Checklist

Checklist Item	Description
Engine	Does the car start without hesitation? Can you hear any squeaking, rattles, knocks or bangs? Do you notice any excessive exhaust smoke when idling or under acceleration? If you have permission from the seller and the necessary skills & tools, check the condition of the spark plugs, they can gives clues as to possible engine issues.
Exterior	Inspect the exterior of the car for any signs of damage or wear and tear. Check for any dents, scratches or rusts. Get underneath the car and look for signs oil; also look for excessive rust, particularly around the sills and on the exhaust.
Interior	Inspect the interior of the car for any signs of wear and tear or damage. Check the seats, carpets and dashboard for any stains or tears.
Features	Check that all the features and equipment are working properly, including the air conditioning, audio system, power windows and mirrors.
Tyres	Check the tyres for tread depth, tread wear and the evenness of wear. Also make sure the tyre walls are not damaged or severely cracked. Make sure the tyres have enough tread for safe driving.
Check the brakes	Check the brakes by driving on a quiet road and testing them at different speeds. Pay attention to the brake pedal feel, the level of resistance and the sound of the brakes. Does the car pull to one side when braking?
Check the steering	Check the steering by making turns at different speeds and on different roads. Pay attention to the steering wheel's responsiveness and the level of effort required to turn it. Is the car tugging to one side?

Checklist Item	Description
Check the suspension	Check the suspension by driving over bumps and uneven surfaces. Pay attention to how the car handles and how comfortable the ride is, any loud knocks when going over speed bumps?
Verify the mileage	Look for signs that the mileage may not be accurate, wear and tear on seats steering wheel and pedals – are they consistent with the mileage? Investigate MOT history and service records/invoices.
Water ingress	Feel around the interior by the sunroof, the footwells and under the carpet in the boot for signs of water ingress. Also look to see if the windows are overly steamed up as this can also be a sign. Damp smells also suggest an issue.
Accessories	Make sure the car has a locking wheel nut key (if applicable) and that a spare wheel and jack, or a tyre inflation kit are included.
Glass	Check that the windscreen and other windows are free from chips, cracks and deep scratches.
Check the oil and fluids	Check the oil level and look under the oil cap, make sure it's not milky. Ensure other fluids are at their recommended levels.

CHAPTER 9:

Buying a Category S or Category N Car

You'll often see cars advertised at a great price that will say Cat S or Cat N, what does that mean and why are they so cheap? Let's take a look.

These cars have been previous written-off by an insurance company. This means they were either stolen, flooded, or involved in an accident where the damage was considered to be too costly to repair by the insurance company, so they paid out the policyholder and kept the salvaged car.

After a write-off, these cars often go into salvage auctions where they purchased by mechanics, body shops, or car dealers, repaired, then re-sold back into the market.

Only two categories of write off are allowed to go back onto the road; these are Cat S and Cat N, which stand for "Structurally Damaged" and "Non-Structurally Damaged" respectively (formerly known as Cat C and Cat D). These categories are assigned to vehicles that have been in accidents and have sustained damage, but they indicate different levels of severity.

A Cat S car is a vehicle that has been declared as structurally damaged by an insurance company. This means that the car has sustained damage to its frame or chassis and it may no longer be considered safe to drive. These cars are typically written off by insurance companies and they can only be returned to the road once they've been repaired.

One major flaw in the rules regarding Cat S cars is that there is currently no legal requirement for the cars to be inspected and judged safe for the road once repaired. For this reason, it can be difficult to know if a written-off Cat S car has been properly repaired and is safe to drive without a full mechanical inspection by a professional.

A Cat N car, on the other hand, is a vehicle that has been declared as non-structurally damaged by an insurance company. This means that the car has sustained "non-structural" damage, but it's not considered to be as severe as with a Cat S car (body panel damage is most likely). These cars can typically be repaired and returned to the road without any major issues.

Please note that Cat A and Cat B cars are not allowed to be returned to the road under any circumstances and some further restrictions apply to those vehicles and even to the use of their parts.

When buying a Cat S or Cat N car, it's important to be aware of the potential risks and to take steps to protect yourself. For the reasons stated before, it's a good idea to have the car inspected by a reputable mechanic before making a purchase to make sure that the repairs have been done properly and that the car is safe to drive.

Cat S and Cat N cars will typically retail at around 20-30% less than a "clean" equivalent vehicle. This means you can grab a bargain but also remember that when you come to sell it your market will be narrower as not everyone will take the chance of a "cat car" and it can also be difficult to part exchange or to sell these vehicles via a used car buying service.

You should be aware that although these cars will typically be priced lower than similar cars that haven't been in accidents, you may have trouble finding a lender willing to finance a Cat S car.

Please also note that not all written-off cars will appear on the register or via some mainstream history checks as insurance companies are not obliged to register their write-offs at the time of writing (although the majority do!). A good vehicle history check service (like Vcheck or Car Vertical for example) can give an idea of the extent of the damage and what repairs have been done as "Category cars" have often gone through a salvage auction and many of these will appear on the history checks along with photos of the vehicle in its pre-repaired state.

Cat S and Cat N cars can, at times, be more problematic to insure and their history should always be disclosed at the outset when obtaining an insurance quotation. It's also worth noting that if the car were to be written off again in future, the potential pay-out would generally be much less than for a car with a clean history.

Some people swear by buying Cat S and Cat N cars as they feel that they're getting a bargain and saving a car from the scrap heap; others wouldn't touch them with a bargepole.

Give some thought about how you would feel about owning one and if the potential for a big discount would temp you or not?

The Auto Trader website has an option to include or exclude Cat S/N cars which can save you a lot of time when conducting your initial searches. Just remember that you still need to do your history check to verify things for yourself.

CHAPTER 10:

Negotiating the Price of a Used Car in the UK

When buying a used car in the UK, negotiating the price is an important step in the process. Whether you're buying from a professional trader or a private seller, being able to negotiate the price can save you money and help you get the best deal possible.

The first step in negotiating the price of a used car is to do your research. Look up the prices of similar cars in your area and determine the fair market value of the car you're interested in. This will give you a starting point for your negotiations and will help you make an informed decision.

Next, it's important to be prepared to negotiate. This means having a clear idea of the price you're willing to pay and being able to justify your offer with the research you've done on the fair market value of the car. Additionally, you should be aware of any potential issues with the car, such as a high mileage, bodywork damage, or a lack of service history. This can give you leverage during negotiations, as the seller may be more willing to lower the price if there are issues with the car.

When negotiating the price, it's important to be polite and professional, many people are aggressive or rude and this is unlikely to ever result in a positive outcome.

Avoid making personal attacks or being confrontational. Instead, focus on the facts and present your case in a calm and logical manner (this needs repairing or replacing, which will cost £X).

It's important to be willing to walk away if the price is not right.

Remember that there are other cars on the market and you should not be afraid of missing out on a deal if the price is not right.

When buying from a professional trader, it's important to be aware that they may have less room to negotiate than a private seller. Professional traders have overhead costs and need to make a profit, so their prices may be higher. However, professional traders may be more willing to negotiate on financing and trade-in options, so it's important to consider these options as well.

Cash is no longer king with professional traders who will likely make a good profit from selling you a finance package, keep this in mind and don't get lead into signing up to something that isn't perfect for you.

The simple rule is if the price is not right, walk away and find something else.

CHAPTER 11:

Car Finance Options

Whilst some people can pay cash for their car there are also several finance options available to buyers.

Please note that I am not a financial advisor or finance professional, this information is for your guidance only; please always consult a qualified finance professional for such financial advice.

Here are three of the most common types of car finance available in the UK:

1. **Hire Purchase (HP):** With this type of finance, you pay an initial deposit followed by monthly instalments over an agreed period, usually between 12 and 60 months. Once all the instalments have been paid, you own the car outright. This type of finance is usually available from car dealerships and finance companies. It's considered a stable option and it's easy to understand, it also allows you to own the car once the payments are finished. However, the interest rates can be higher than other options and the car's value depreciates while you are making payments.

2. **Personal Contract Purchase (PCP):** This type of finance is similar to Hire Purchase and Leasing, but with a few key differences. With PCP, you pay an initial deposit and then monthly instalments over an agreed period, usually between 12 and 36 months. At the end of the agreement, you have the option to return the car, keep the car by paying the final balloon payment, or trade the car in for a new one. It allows you to keep your options open, you can return the car, keep it or trade it in. However, it's important to keep an eye on the mileage and the final balloon payment can be high. This kind of finance is

very popular with car dealers as it gives the impression of low payments and makes it very easy for them to move you into another car at any stage. It can be an expensive way to buy or lease a vehicle.

3. **Personal Contract Hire / Leasing (PCH):** This is a type of car leasing, where you pay a fixed monthly amount for the use of a car over an agreed period, usually between 12 and 48 months. At the end of the agreement, you return the car to the lender. This type of finance is usually available from car dealerships and finance companies. It's considered a flexible option as it allows you to change cars more frequently and you don't have to worry about the car's depreciation or maintenance costs. However, you don't own the car and you will have to return it at the end of the agreement and if you exceed the mileage limit or if there is damage to the car, you will be charged extra fees. Whilst it's possible to lease a used car the value, at least in my opinion, seems to be in new vehicle leasing which can be much cheaper than you might think (sometimes cheaper than a PCP lease on a used car). You could argue that it makes sense to own appreciating assets and to rent depreciating ones!

4. **Bank Loan:** This is slightly different to the other options as its secured against you rather than the vehicle. This means the car has no finance against it so can be sold at any time without the need to settle the loan first, you could then reinvest into another car or something else – if you keep making those payments of course!

Each option has its own pros and cons and it's important to weigh them up carefully before deciding. Additionally, it's always a good idea to shop around and compare offers from different lenders (perhaps using a comparison site) and different dealerships. When choosing the right car finance option for you, it's important to consider your budget, how long you plan to keep the car and whether you want to own the car or not.

Use care and common sense

There are a variety of sales techniques that car dealers in the UK may use to lure people into car finance, even those who have clearly stated that they want to pay cash. In my opinion some of these techniques and tactics are bordering on unethical but you can, I'm sure, form your own opinion.

Some of these could include:

1. Low monthly payments: Car dealers may advertise low monthly payments to make financing a car seem more affordable despite the fact that lower cost or better value payment terms may be available.

2. Limited-time offers or "other interest": Car dealers may use limited-time offers or the spectre of another interested party to create a sense of urgency and pressure customers into making a decision.

3. Add-ons and upgrades: Car dealers may offer add-ons and upgrades, such as extended warranties, insurances, or service plans, to increase the overall cost of the sale. It has been known for unscrupulous dealers to throw these extras in "for free" but the cost is added to the finance amount!

4. Pushy salespeople: Some car dealers may employ pushy salespeople who use high-pressure tactics to get customers to sign on the dotted line.

5. Focusing on the monthly payment rather than the total cost: Car dealers may focus on the monthly payment rather than the total cost of the car, which can make the financing seem more affordable.

6. Not disclosing all the terms of the finance or the interest rate or giving them to you in a bundle of paperwork that they hope you won't read through.

Not every car salesperson is pushy or greedy and there are some great salespeople around who offer a superb service to their clients. Just remember that it's a hard industry that is fuelled by commissions and very tough targets.

Always go into the dealership prepared and never sign up for something there and then without conducting your research. Smoke and mirrors are widely used by car dealers to lure people into finance agreements such as "dealer contributions" or extra services offered that are only available for those taking finance. Always question the ethics and motives of these "amazing deals" and always do the sums yourself and compare what else is available to you from elsewhere.

Not everyone in the world is trying to rip you off or unfairly profit from you, not is every car dealer, there are some great ones out there but there are also a few sharks!

.

CHAPTER 12:

Think about ULEZ

ULEZ stands for "Ultra Low Emission Zone" and is a designated area where vehicles must meet certain emissions standards in order to be driven within the zone. The ULEZ standards are more stringent than the national standards and vehicles that do not meet the standards must pay a daily charge to drive within the zone. The ULEZ was first introduced in London in April 2019 and is currently in operation 24 hours a day, 7 days a week.

The London ULEZ is likely to expand in the future, with plans for it to be expanded to the entire Greater London area and to other major UK cities in the coming years.

The expansion of ULEZ is part of a wider effort to improve air quality in the UK by reducing emissions from vehicles. It is expected that the expansion of ULEZ will encourage people to switch to lower-emitting vehicles and will help to reduce the number of premature deaths caused by air pollution in the UK. Let's not forget that it will also raise a lot of revenue for the Government of course...

I would encourage anyone reading this to serious reconsider buying a non-ULEZ exempt vehicle as, even if your town is not currently affected by this, it may be soon and the value of your vehicle could plummet in future as ULEZ becomes more widespread or further, harsher, restrictions are imposed.

This book is not about ULEZ so you can do some further reading online if you so wish, the hope here is that you at least give this some consideration before buying your next car.

CHAPTER 13:

Common Used Car Scams

The used car market in the UK is generally a reputable one, but unfortunately, there are still some scammers out there who try to take advantage of buyers.

Used car scams have been a long-standing problem in the UK according to the Citizens Advice Bureau and the National Trading Standards (NTS).

Here are some commonly used car scams to be aware of:

1. **Clocking:** This is when a seller alters the odometer reading to make it appear as though the car has lower mileage than it does. This is illegal in the UK and it can significantly affect the value of the car – it's also rife!

2. **Curbsiders:** These are individuals who pose as private sellers but are unlicensed dealers. They may have a variety of cars on offer and they may not disclose important information about the car's history or condition. They hide their identity as motor traders so that the buyer is not given the benefit of protections they would normally have buying from a dealer. This is often done in order to sell a "lemon" or simply to avoid comeback.

3. **Flood or accident-damaged "Cat" cars:** Some sellers may try to conceal the fact that a car has been in a flood or an accident. This can significantly affect the car's performance and safety, so it's important to be aware of any signs of damage, such as mismatched paint or body panel gaps that aren't aligned properly. Beware of the term "HPI Clear" and <u>always</u> conduct your own history checks.

4. **Cloning:** This is when a seller takes the Vehicle Identification Number (VIN) or Registration Number from a legally registered and legitimate car and uses it to register a stolen or salvage car. It's important to check the VIN number and the registration documents to make sure they match.

5. **Money transfer scams:** This is when a seller asks the buyer to transfer the money for the car before they've even seen the car. This is a red flag and a common scam, as it allows the seller to take the money and disappear without providing the car.

6. **Warranty scams:** This is when a seller offers a warranty for the car, but it turns out to be fake or the seller doesn't honour the warranty. It's important to thoroughly research the warranty and the seller before making a decision and to be aware of any red flags such as a low price or a lack of documentation.

7. **Fake service history:** Fake service history can be difficult to detect, but it's important to be aware of the signs, such as a lack of documentation or inconsistencies in the service records. It's also important to be aware of red flags, such as a low price or a lack of information from the seller. One way to verify the service history of a used car is by checking the car's service book, which is usually found in the glove compartment. The service book should have stamps and signatures of the services that have been done on the car, including the date, the mileage and the service type. Service stamps are extremely easy to forge and the practice is widespread so feel free to contact the dealers noted on the stamps to verify the information for yourself. Also see if there are lots of receipts for the servicing and repairs that are claimed to have been carried out. Another way to verify the service history is by contacting the previous owners. Additionally, having a professional mechanic inspect the car can also help reveal any issues with the car's maintenance history.

8. **Too good to be true:** this involves the seller advertising a vehicle at a very low price, but then asking the buyer to pay an additional sum, such as transportation or import fees, before the car can be delivered. In some cases, the car may not exist or may be significantly different from the one described in the ad. This is one of the most common scams in the UK at the time of writing.

It's important to be aware of these scams, do your research and take your time when buying a used car.

The NTS suggests that consumers should be cautious when buying a used car and to take steps to protect themselves such as:

- Researching the vehicle and the seller before making a purchase

- Checking the vehicle's registration and history before buying

- Visiting the vehicle in person before buying

- Having a mechanic inspect the vehicle before buying

- Pay by credit card, if possible, as this can give you additional protection under section 75 of the Consumer Credit Act

Not everyone is looking to rip you off, but you should always use caution and understand the importance of evidence over words!

CHAPTER 14:

Where to find the best deals

There are various places to find a used car deal, from small high street traders through to huge online car supermarkets, but beware, there are also potential pitfalls with each that I will try to address here.

Buying a car used to always be a face-to-face transaction and always involved a test-drive. Since the start of COVID-19 restrictions, many car dealerships have added a fully online sales option to their box of tricks, this allows you to view and buy a car online and then have it delivered to your home or workplace. If you don't like the car, you have a brief window that you can return it in and obtain a refund.

Let's look at the main options and try to identify why you may or may not wish to each of them.

Traditional Car Auctions

Most UK car auctions these days are for trade buyers only and therefore not open to the public. Buying from auction is not for the feint hearted as cars are generally sold "as seen" and you usually have only basic information to help you in deciding if this is the car for you. Auctions generally take place both in person at a physical auction site and online, although several auction sites moved to online only operations at the beginning of the pandemic.

There are lots of different auctions in the UK, from Classic Car auctions to Police Auctions (yes, you can buy an ex-Police car) to mainstream trade auctions such as BCA and Manheim who are generally selling part-exchanges, ex-lease, ex-company fleet and car buying service cars (WeBuyAnyCar etc) back into the trade. Traders will also sometimes use these auctions to get rid of troublesome stock or cars that are not selling.

In my personal opinion, unless you're mechanically minded and experienced, I think the auction is best left to the trade.

Salvage Auctions

The most familiar one of these is Copart which offers mostly written-off Cat S/Cat N cars that are yet to be repaired. You REALLY know what you're getting yourself into if you're buying a damaged vehicle, so this is only for the experts amongst you.

Online Auction Sites

Yes, we're talking about eBay and the like.

Buying a car on eBay in the UK can be a good idea if you do your research and take the necessary precautions. Here are some pros and cons to consider:

Pros:

- You can often find a wider selection of cars on an auction site than you would at a local dealership.

- You may be able to find a better deal on an auction site than you would at a dealership.

- You can see the seller's feedback and ratings before making a purchase, which can give you an idea of the seller's reliability.

Cons:

- It can be harder to verify the condition of a car when buying online.

- It can be harder to negotiate the price of a car on an auction site than it would be in person.

- You will need to arrange for the car to be shipped or picked up, which can add to the cost.

- These kinds of sites are known to attract scammers.

Online Classifieds

This would be websites like Auto Trader, Motors.co.uk, Gumtree etc.

These websites attract both trade and private sellers of varying qualities, from your next door neighbour, to a small time car trader to a full franchised dealership.

My "go to" would be Auto Trader which is packed with car ads and has a very easy to use interface for filtering results to your liking. It's not a cheap platform to advertise on so perhaps doesn't attract quite as many bottom feeders are the sites that are free to place and advert on.

Large Online Dealers

These are dealers who exist only in the online space, companies like Cinch and Cazoo.

They generally have no showrooms but offer comprehensive images and details of any damage on their website. You pay a small amount for delivery and have the option to return the car if it is not to your liking. The idea is to sell large volumes of used cars at competitive prices whilst cutting out a lot of costs associated with traditional franchised dealerships.

Franchised Dealerships

This would be your local main dealer (Audi, Jaguar, BMW, Renault, Ford etc) often part of large groups such as Marshall, Evans Halshaw or Arnold Clark. Here you can buy "approved used" vehicles which may benefit from a better warranty than those you would find at an independent dealer. You also have the additional safety belt of being able to complain to the manufacturer if the local dealer falls short in any way. Prices can be more expensive at a franchised dealer but an approved used car should have undergone extensive pre-sale checks and will usually come with a host of benefits that you wouldn't usually expect to find elsewhere. Part-exchange is almost always available.

Keep in mind that main dealers will almost always be every bit as selling you a bunch of add-on products and services as they are in selling you a car, more on this in the next chapter.

Don't buy from one of these thinking you'll be getting a better car or better service than anywhere else though, they just may be able to offer a level of warranty that others can't. As the old saying goes, always

INSPECT and don't EXPECT (evidence>words). I would do the same checks when buying from a main dealer as I would buying from a small trader selling from their home.

I've personally only purchased from a main dealer twice in my life, once was the worst car buying experience I've ever had, the second time was way below average. I paid cash both times and felt a bit like a second class citizen for not filling their coffers with car finance commissions.

Independent Dealerships

The size and quality of these dealerships can vary, they usually source vehicles from auction or from main dealer part-exchanges, they tidy the cars up, often put a new MOT on them and a short warranty (usually a third-party warranty). Part-exchange is almost always available.

The benefit here is that you can go and view the car and test drive it before you buy it – *I bet it's got no more than a tablespoon of fuel in it though, lol!*

Small Traders

Often working from home, quality can obviously vary but I've had some great experiences dealing with small, home-based operators. Don't expect dealership facilities and obviously their range of finance and warranty options may be more limited than with some.

Some of these guys will work harder and provide a better service as they don't have a flash showroom whilst others will do the exact opposite for the same reason.

Part-exchange is often available.

Social Media

Be careful here, there are of course good genuine people selling cars here but also a fair number of scammers and unscrupulous sellers. Proceed with extreme caution and you may unearth a genuine bargain.

Online Forums & Car Clubs

Although not really any different than buying from a private seller, many people frequenting forums are more interested in their cars than most which means they may well have treated their pride and joy to a five star experience and have a folder full of evidence to prove it. You can often see their previous posts too and find out if the car has been a dream to live with or a bit of a nightmare as well as learning about any modifications that may have been carried out.

Forums and clubs usually have a classified ads section and a "Wanted" section so may well be worth a look.

TIP! : Remember the advice on car history checks, just because you see a green tick or "HPI Clear" on a trusted website or from a main dealer, it doesn't mean that you shouldn't also conduct your own checks. The systems used by many dealers to check their stock history are not as comprehensive as the ones used by the likes of you or me.

CHAPTER 15:

Add-on products and services

Car Dealerships love to sell add-ons, these are a range of products and services designed to be tagged on to your car purchase once the transaction is being finalised.

Many of these services have a great deal of merit but it's not always advisable to buy them from a dealer, always shop around to find the best deal for you!

Let's look at some of these services and what they are designed to do.

GAP Insurance

Also known as Guaranteed Asset Protection (GAP) insurance.

Cars can lose a significant amount of value in the first few years of ownership and gap insurance can provide protection against this depreciation in the event of a total loss (write-off).

If a car is stolen or declared a total loss due to an accident, gap insurance can help to cover the difference between the actual cash value of the vehicle and the remaining balance on the car finance or lease agreement.

This can be a wise investment but dealerships sometimes charge way more than the market rate for this cover so it may pay to shop around. They will sometimes "throw it in" as part of your finance package, this is sometimes a sign that you're perhaps paying too much for your finance.

Ceramic Coating / Paint Protection

This is a process that should be carried out by an experienced car detailer, usually after paint correction has taken place.

Ceramic coating can protect a car's paint from the effects of UV rays, acid rain and other environmental factors that can cause damage over time and can make a car's paint more durable and resistant to scratches, chips and other types of damage.

It's important to note that ceramic coating is not a permanent solution and it may require maintenance, but it can provide an added level of protection for your car's paint.

It's a nice thing to have done on the right car but again, pricing is key as is the quality of the work. There may be some value in getting this done by a reputable car detailer than a car dealership as it's not something to be left in the hands of a novice.

Interior Protection / Scotch guarding

A similar process to ceramic coating can be carried out on the car interior, carpets and upholstery. It may be worth considering if you have young children or pets that will be travelling in the car.

As always, weigh up your options elsewhere before checking that box with the car dealer as you may find that a professional valeter or detailer can offer a better service at a lower price.

Extended Warranties

These vary massively in terms of their scope of cover and the excess (deductible) applied to certain types of claim. There are full parts and labour warranties that cover just about anything that may happen to your car, down to cheap warranties that will offer you £500 if your engine fails. It's very important to understand exactly what the warranty does and does not cover before purchasing, also read online reviews if it is a third-party warranty. Don't be blinded by big names like AA and RAC, do the research yourself.

Service Plans

Straightforward enough, it covers the cost of scheduled maintenance and repairs for a set period. Service plans typically only cover scheduled maintenance and repairs and may not cover all types of repairs or damage.

This may seem cheap but is it being added to your car finance? It may be costing you more than you think if so.

Also consider if this is transferable if you sell the car; if it's not and your circumstances change you could have just flushed some cash down the drain.

It's important to carefully consider whether you need these add-ons and upgrades, as they can add to the overall cost of the car. It's also a good idea to compare prices and check for any discounts before making a purchase.

CHAPTER 16:

Used Car Buying Checklist

Here is a used car buying checklist that can help you make an informed and confident purchase:

Checklist Item	Description
Research the car	Research the make and model of the car you are interested in and check its reliability, safety ratings, and fuel economy.
Research car finance deals	Research different car finance options such as car loans, leases and personal loans, compare the interest rates, terms and conditions and choose the one that suits you best.
Check the vehicle history	Check the vehicle history report to verify the mileage, check for outstanding finance and check that the car has has not been written-off or stolen.
Inspecting and testing the car	Inspect and test the car following the Used Car Inspection checklist in Chapter 8 – take time to do this thoroughly.
Check the service history	Ask the seller for the car's service history and check if the car has been well maintained. Verify the history with invoices or by calling the dealerships noted on the service stamps.
Have a mechanic inspect the car	Have a qualified mechanic inspect the car to check for any potential issues or repairs that may be needed.

Checklist Item	Description
Negotiate the price	Negotiate the price with the seller and take into account the car's condition, mileage and service history.
Check the paperwork	Check that all the paperwork is in order, including the registration, MOT certificate and service history.
Check the warranty	Check if the car comes with a warranty and ask about the terms and conditions.
Check the insurance cost	Check the insurance cost for the car you are interested in and compare it to other similar cars.
Close the deal	Once you are satisfied with the car, the financing and have completed all the necessary checks, close the deal and make the purchase.

CHAPTER 17:

Sell or Part Exchange? (BONUS CHAPTER)

We've talked a lot about buying a car but what are you going to do with the old one?

When it comes to your existing vehicle you really have two major decisions to make, are you prepared to sell it yourself or do you want to part-exchange the car.

Selling your car privately can be a great way to get the most money for your vehicle. When you sell your car privately, you have the freedom to set your own price and negotiate with potential buyers. Additionally, you can advertise your car in a variety of ways, such as online classifieds or local listings, to reach a wide audience. However, selling your car privately can be time-consuming, frustrating and may require significant effort on your part. You'll need to take care of all the paperwork and legal requirements and have to deal with the possibility of fraud or scam attempts.

Part-exchanging your car with a dealer can be a much more convenient option. When you part exchange your car, you're essentially trading it in for a new vehicle. This means that you won't have to go through the hassle of advertising and selling your car and you'll be able to walk away with a new vehicle in your driveway. The downside of a part-exchange is that you may not get as much money for your car when you part exchange it. Dealers typically offer less than the market value of a vehicle in order to be able to make a profit on your vehicle when they send it to auction, sell it to another trader, or sell it on to a retail customer.

There is another option however and that's using a car buying service. Notable car buyers include companies like WeBuyAnyCar (WBAC), Motorway and CarWow, but there are several more national and local services that will offer a quick way of turning your car into cash.

WBAC

This is a very popular service, you simply pop your registration number into the website along with some very basic details and WBAC gives you an indicative price that they would be willing to pay for your vehicle. If you're happy with the amount you can then take the car to a local centre to have it inspected (for a fee); once the inspection is complete they will make their formal offer (or even refuse to offer if they find something they don't like). The final offer may be higher or lower than the online estimated price depending on the condition of the car and the presence of things like service records, documentation, accessories and the car having the number of keys etc.

Motorway (and similar)

The likes of Motorway and CarWow work slightly differently as they are basically a portal for traders to bid on your car. You will be required to take a lot of quote specific photos of your car and any damage to it. The traders will then bid on the car; you will then choose whether to accept or decline the offers. The buyer then agrees a time to collect the car from you.

How to ensure you get the best price possible when selling your car

Make sure the car is impeccably clean, get a valeter or professional car cleaner to give the car a really good exterior and interior clean. Do this before listing it for sale or showing it to a car buying service.

Make sure you get all your documentation together (maybe put it into a file), MOT's, V5, service history, receipts/invoices. Keep it all together and have it to hand.

If the car has any small areas of damage, consider getting a quote from a smart repair service to put these right, scuffs and scrapes to the car bodywork or alloy wheels can really affect people's perceptions of a car and repairs may cost less than you think.

Ensure any photographs are taken in a good location with plenty of light, look at professional car adverts and try to mimic the style of the photos and make sure to include things like photos of the service history, of the open boot, one of the dash (including the odometer) and photos of the wheels. These can not only show the car in its best light but also save a lot of time handling enquiries.

Try and find that spare key as 2 keys are better than one!

Finally, be honest, tell people truthfully about any faults, damage, or issues. If people discover faults for themselves, they will try to use them to knock down the price or may even think that you're hiding things from them and walk away.

CHAPTER 18:

...and finally

That's all folks!

We've covered everything from how to properly inspect a used car before purchasing, to negotiating a deal.

By following the tips and advice outlined in this guide, I hope you can feel more confident when buying a used car and that it helps to ensure that you are getting a reliable, high-quality vehicle that fits your needs and budget.

Remember to do your research, take your time and trust your instincts when it comes to buying a used car, it's my sincere hope that if you follow this guide, it should help you to drive away happy with your new purchase.

My final thought is probably a familiar one - If something seems too good to be true, it almost always is.

Thanks so much for reading; I hope I didn't go on too much...if you enjoyed it, please tell your friends and leave a nice review.

Jim

Twitter @notaguru3

Facebook @DefinitelyNotAGuru

Instagram @notagurujim

YouTube @DefinitelyNotAGuru

Website : https://notaguru.co.uk

Printed in Great Britain
by Amazon